Startup Stories
Lessons Learned from a Startup's Launch, Grind, and Growth

Jordan Raynor

Startup Stories

Amazon.com Best Seller
#1 in Christian Business
#2 in Startups
#3 in Innovation

Copyright © 2014 by Jordan Raynor

All rights reserved. No part of this publication may be reproduced, distributed, or transmitted in any form or by any means, including photocopying, recording, or other electronic or mechanical methods, without the prior written permission of the publisher, except in the case of brief quotations embodied in critical reviews and certain other noncommercial uses permitted by copyright law. For permission requests, write to the publisher at jordan@jordanraynor.com.

ISBN: 9781499573916

*Dedicated to Ellison and Kaylin
as you each start new chapters of your own stories*

Table of Contents

Dedication 3

Introduction 7

Part One: Launching 11

    Chapter 1: Solve real problems 13

    Chapter 2: Choose your startup spouse wisely 17

    Chapter 3: Ideas are cheap 23

    Chapter 4: Start with stories 27

    Chapter 5: Stay focused on what matters 31

    Chapter 6: Be comfortable in your own skin 37

    Chapter 7: Be flexible 41

Part Two: Grinding 45

    Chapter 8: Bet the farm 47

    Chapter 9: If they don't tell you yes, they are telling you no 51

    Chapter 10: If it seems too good to be true, it is 57

    Chapter 11: Raise money from friends and family with caution 61

    Chapter 12: Startups are emotional roller coasters 65

    Chapter 13: Startups are a young person's game 71

Part Three: Growing 77

    Chapter 14: Domain knowledge matters 79

    Chapter 15: Take advantage of being unknown 83

    Chapter 16: Stay humble and accessible 89

    Chapter 17: Rely heavily on interns 93

Chapter 18: Have the audacity to ask 97

Chapter 19: Don't sell products, tell stories 101

Chapter 20: Stand for something 107

Epilogue 113

Acknowledgements 115

About the Author 117

Introduction

This book is for anyone who has ever dreamed of starting something. Maybe you have lots of great ideas but no clue as to how to bring them to life. Maybe you know how to get your idea to launch but you're not sure "startup life" is right for you. Maybe you're an entrepreneur like me, looking to commiserate over the brutality that is the road called entrepreneurship. Maybe you're interested in how technology startups are changing politics and government. Or maybe you're just curious why people choose a fancy-sounding French word to describe a quality that to some degree lives in most of us – the desire to create.

    I haven't always thought of myself as an entrepreneur, but looking back over the course of my short life (I'm 27 as I write this), that label is probably the best way to describe my lifelong passion for creating. I started my first "business" when I was nine years old, selling baseball cards out of my bedroom. It was a terrible business as my customer acquisition strategy was completely reliant on how hospitable my parents were feeling. In the eighth grade, my entrepreneurial spirit took a different shape as I watched the 2000 election, mesmerized by the romanticism that characterizes the launch, rise, and fall of presidential campaigns. Planning on launching a campaign for President of the United States in 2024 (self-confidence was not an issue for me), I started my career down a political path, taking my first "real job" at the age of 17 managing a countywide campaign in Hillsborough County, Florida (in my hometown of Tampa). Winning that campaign made me think I was addicted to politics. Years later, I realized that it wasn't politics I was addicted to; it was launching things that mattered and winning.

I started my first (real) business, Direct Media Strategies, in 2009 – an "online communications agency" that helped political campaigns, causes, and corporations use the Internet to win. A year into that business, I had more than quadrupled what I was making in my first job out of college; but more importantly, I was having the time of my life because I had found my calling – launching companies. In 2011, Direct Media Strategies was "acquihired" by Engage – deemed a "mega interactive agency" by Mashable. A little more than a year later, I was ready to start up again.

My next startup – Citizinvestor – is a central character in this book. You've probably never heard of Citizinvestor before. That's OK. It is just one of the more than 6,000,000 companies started in the United States in 2012, according to Forbes.com. Citizinvestor hasn't been acquired for a billion dollars and it doesn't have a story of dramatic failure. Currently valued at $3,500,000, our startup, like many others, lies somewhere in the middle.

You'll learn much more about Citizinvestor in the stories that make up this short book. Each chapter shares a lesson I believe is critical for any entrepreneur to learn. Most of these lessons are told through stories of our experience at Citizinvestor, but they are applicable to almost any business. In that respect, this isn't really a story about our relatively unknown startup. It isn't even a story about me. These are stories that convey valuable lessons I've learned about what it takes to launch a company, grind through startup life, and grow a business from the ground up.

I am constantly asked to share the lessons I've learned as a young entrepreneur. That's why I wrote this book. While I've certainly done a lot right, I've unquestionably done more wrong. I hope this book helps you avoid some of the mistakes I've made and provides some valuable tips and encouragement for your entrepreneurial endeavors.

Finally, to join the conversation surrounding this book on social media, be sure to use #StartupStories.

PART ONE
Launching

Solve real problems
Choose your startup spouse wisely
Ideas are cheap
Start with stories Stay focused on what matters
Be comfortable in your own skin
Be flexible

Chapter 1: Solve real problems

I had done this enough times that I had come to expect the pre-speech nerves I was now feeling. But this was a whole new level. Before I took the stage, I was able to calm my nerves long enough to appreciate the moment I was living. In a few minutes, I was to take the stage following an amazing "fireside chat" with Chris Hughes, a Co-founder of Facebook and the leader of the Obama campaign's historic "My Barack Obama" social network. If that wasn't cool enough, the rest of the lineup of speakers at the event included the CEOs of The New York Times, The Guardian, and Tumblr; the CTO of Amazon.com; a General Partner of Andreessen Horowitz, and a former United States Senator.

And then there was me, Jordan Raynor, a Co-founder of a company no one could properly pronounce. To say I was out of my league would be an epic understatement. As a friend of mine said to me a few days before the speech, "Dude, I think you're great and all, but you have no business being on that stage."

My friend was right. So how did this happen?

Mostly through grace. In my short career as an entrepreneur, I have been blessed immeasurably with amazing opportunities I did not earn or deserve. But as I inched closer to the edge of my seat, ready to charge the podium, I couldn't help but think that one of the reasons I was there was because the team at our young startup had decided to solve a *real* problem.

Nineteen months prior to that speech, a professional acquaintance of mine by the name of Tony DeSisto emailed me, as his subject line stated, a "quick question" about a "revolutionary idea" he wanted to share with me. I didn't know Tony well, but I love hearing people pitch ideas for startups, so I asked Tony if he could meet me at my office the following afternoon. Little did I know how great of an impact that "quick question" would have on my life.

As we sat across from each other at my cheap conference table, Tony started in on his pitch. After losing his race for the Tampa City Council a year prior, Tony was appointed to the City of Tampa's Budget Advisory Committee. On the surface, this seemed like the worst consolation prize of all time; but in fact, it was a blessing in disguise. Tony explained that the City of Tampa had hundreds of projects that were "shovel-ready" but weren't being completed simply due to a lack of funding. This had always been a problem, but one that was greatly exacerbated by the Great Recession. Tony argued that, if given the opportunity, citizens would step up to donate to the public projects they cared about most. Essentially, they would be able to earmark their dollars to a specific government project. "It's basically Kickstarter for government," he said, referring to the rapidly growing crowdfunding website.

I was immediately smitten with the audacity of the problem Tony wanted to solve. Government entities *never* have enough financial resources to provide every project and service that citizens want. Up until that point, there was no real solution to the problem aside from raising taxes. But allowing citizens to pick and choose which parks, playgrounds, or pools they wanted to donate to? *That* was a powerful idea to solve a very real problem facing cities across the globe.

We are living at a time of unprecedented growth in the number of people starting companies. It has never been easier to be an entrepreneur. But starting a company is easy. Solving a real problem is insanely hard. It seems like every day we see the launch of a new social media application or wearable hardware device. These startups may be cool and fun, and some of them will make obscene amounts of money, but are they solving important problems?

Tony and I were once invited to a startup pitch competition hosted by the famous SXSW technology conference. We were competing against companies in the "Innovative World Technologies" category and we ended up losing to three PhDs from Stanford who were trying to "create sustainable natural lighting" by developing a DNA sequence that made plants glow. Yes glow, not grow. When a reporter asked me if I was disappointed that we lost the competition, I said, "We lost to a glowing plant. I don't think I can be disappointed about that." Talk about solving a real problem!

Conventional business wisdom says that it doesn't matter what your startup produces, so long as it's profitable. But I believe we are seeing a rising tide of founders who are challenging that wisdom and are building startups that are both profitable *and* solving real, important problems. I'm convinced that this is a key ingredient to our success at Citizinvestor. We have chosen to take on an important problem facing every government and citizen. By focusing on a problem of such great importance, we have gained access to more amazing people and opportunities in two years than most people get in a lifetime. We have been invited to The White House to talk about what implications crowdfunding might have on the federal government;

we were featured alongside a movie with Matt Damon; we were flown to France to address the Council of Europe; we had tea with the Lieutenant Governor of California. Even if Citizinvestor were to fail, the experiences we have had along the way would have made it all worthwhile. I believe these experiences are a direct result of us tackling a significant problem.

Every company solves a problem. That's what customers are paying for. Amazon solves the problem of having to get in the car to drive to the store. Google is solving the problem of organizing the world's information. TOMS is solving the problem of children not having shoes. What problem do you want to solve? My advice to you is simple: Find a real problem that, if you solve it, will create maximum profit *and* impact. If you focus on what matters, you will build a great business, create change, and gain access to amazing people and opportunities along the way.

Chapter 2: Choose your startup spouse wisely

As my plane descended into Nashua, New Hampshire, the snow-covered ground was a stark reminder that I was not in Tampa anymore. It was January 2008, just days before New Hampshire's presidential primary. I had come to the Granite State to witness history, having signed up to volunteer for John McCain in this do-or-die contest for his bid for the presidency. Over the next few days, I would witness two surprises that would have dramatic ramifications on American politics for the next decade: Hillary Clinton's upset victory over Barack Obama, and John McCain's win which propelled him to capturing the Republican Party's nomination for President of the United States. But more significant for me personally was the surprise that I would meet my future business partner while trekking through a postcard-worthy New Hampshire winter.

Once off the plane, I immediately phoned Mark Sharpe who was meeting me at the airport. Mark had been my eighth-grade American Government teacher and my first boss (his was the campaign I ran at the age of 17); but on this trip, Mark would play matchmaker, introducing me to my future startup spouse.

"Just a heads up, a guy by the name of Tony DeSisto may be crashing with us in our hotel room," Mark told me.

In retrospect, this first meeting of Tony and myself seems quite fitting. We had both been brought to New Hampshire by the allure of a bootstrapped presidential campaign that operated a lot like a startup. We shared a romanticism for politics and government uncommon among people our age. And, perhaps most poignantly, it appeared that we would be "crashing" together in a cheap hotel room, a perfect foretelling of the Airbnb places we would stay in four years later while gallivanting across the country pitching Citizinvestor.

Before founding Citizinvestor, I had heard that in a startup, your relationship with your Co-founder is a lot like your relationship with your spouse. Having experienced multiple business partnerships over the course of my career, I couldn't agree more.

Making the decision to marry Kara Goskie is the best and most important decision I have ever made (save putting my hope of salvation in Jesus Christ). At the deepest level, I have found in Kara a lifelong partner who shares my values, my dreams, and my ambitions. When selecting a startup spouse, you are looking for those same things! Over the four years I got to know Tony from our meeting in New Hampshire to our launch of Citizinvestor, I learned a lot about him. I knew he shared my values of faith, family, and hard work. I knew we shared similar dreams of using technology to solve real problems in politics and government. And with the birth of our first child Citizinvestor (funny name for a kid, I know), our ambitions were aligned.

While the alignment of values, dreams, and ambitions is critical, it isn't always enough to make for a great startup marriage. You and your Co-founder are about to embark on a (hopefully) long-term relationship with each other, sharing meals, hotel rooms, cramped office space, and everything in between. It's critical that you take the time on the front end to learn as much as you can about each other before entering into a marriage-like relationship. Here are five questions I would recommend you ponder when considering your choice of a startup spouse:

- **Do I have fun hanging out with this person?** If it wasn't for Tony's and my mutual affinity for Chinese buffets, Taylor Swift, and books, our experience working on Citizinvestor wouldn't be nearly as enjoyable or fruitful.
- **Is this person in the same stage of life as I am? If not, how will that impact our working relationship?** When we started working on Citizinvestor, Tony and I were 27 and 25 respectively, but we both acted as if we were at least 15 years older. Tony had two kids and a third on the way. I was married, relatively settled down, with a bedtime of roughly 9:45. We were old men who understood each other's stage of life.
- **Does this person have a similar work ethic and style as I do?** There's nothing Tony and I hate more than tardiness. We would have big problems if one of us was notoriously late for meetings. It also helps that we both like to work relatively "normal" hours, unlike many startup founders who work all night and wake up at 11:00 a.m.
- **Does this person offer a skill set that is complementary to yours?** To say Tony was technologically illiterate when we started working on Citizinvestor is an understatement. But that was OK. I had brought to the table my experience as a tech entrepreneur, while Tony

brought invaluable domain expertise in working with local government entities.
- **Can you speak the truth (kindly) to this person and have difficult conversations with them?** Great relationships allow for both parties to call each other out when appropriate and keep each other accountable. This is a critical quality in any potential business partner as you will undoubtedly need to say tough things to each other for the good of your child (business).

Signing Citizinvestor legal docs with Tony in the parking lot of our favorite Chinese buffet

I realize I'm setting the bar high for what to look for in a startup spouse, but I would strongly encourage you to keep your standards elevated. To be honest, I did not think to consider many of these things when embarking on past business partnerships. I wish I had. It would have saved me a lot of angst. Like marriage, when your relationship with your business partner is bad, it's terrible; when it's good, it's amazing.

Former Citizinvestor intern Daniel Kahn once told me, "You and Tony are like an old married couple." Although an odd way to put it, I realized he was right and that I am incredibly lucky to have found such a great Co-founder "match" at Citizinvestor. But you don't have to rely on luck to find the right startup spouse for you. Use the advice outlined here and take the time to ensure you are making a decision you will be happy with for the rest of your startup's life.

Chapter 3: Ideas are cheap

Before Tony ever pitched me the idea for Citizinvestor, he asked me one of the most common questions I hear from first-time entrepreneurs. He asked if he should be requiring people to sign a Non-Disclosure Agreement (NDA) before talking about the idea that would become Citizinvestor. I told Tony that I had signed dozens of NDAs before, and that I was happy to sign his. But over time, I came to realize how ridiculously silly NDAs are.

Dictionary.com defines an NDA as "a contract whereby one promises to treat information confidentially and not give out information without proper authorization." Typically, entrepreneurs with zero to little legal experience find NDA templates online, print them out, and ask their friends to sign them. You can guess how effective these canned legal documents are. Tony is an attorney, for Pete's sake, and this is the NDA he had me sign:

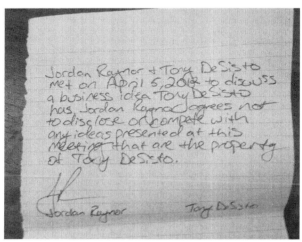

The most bootlegged NDA in the history of startups

While there has been much debate on the efficacy of NDAs, I'm not a lawyer and thus will not challenge the legal impact of these documents. But if you're spending a lot of time protecting the idea for your startup, I will challenge you to question whether or not you're the right entrepreneur to make your idea a success.

Ideas are cheap. We all know someone who has claimed to have had the same idea for a product that is now being built and sold by someone else. How much is that idea worth to the person who failed to execute it? Zilch. Even the greatest ideas are worthless without greater execution. Some great businesses start with great ideas, but the idea isn't the foundation. The foundations of great businesses are great entrepreneurs who are able to execute ideas better than anyone else in the market. These entrepreneurs are confident that they have the experience and drive that make them the most qualified person in the world to turn that idea into a great company. If you are overly protective of your idea, worried that someone might "steal it" and execute it better than you, then maybe you're not the best person to build that business.

A few years ago, a family friend emailed me asking to meet up for coffee to discuss an idea he had for a new business. He was coy about what the idea was, offering zero details that would help me prepare for the meeting. I showed up to Starbucks before my friend and grabbed a chair at the end of the community table. Before my friend sat down, he looked behind him as if he was being hunted by a team of FBI agents. Once settled into his seat, he lowered his head and voice and started in on his pitch. By the way he was acting, I thought he was about to share nuclear launch codes. Instead, he shared a business idea that was nowhere near innovative and certainly didn't deserve the cloak-and-dagger treatment it was receiving. As I began poking holes in the idea, trying desperately to steer my friend away from pursuing the venture, I noticed that he was growing increasingly nervous. It was as if he could feel the FBI agents closing in on him.

"I don't like the way that guy is looking at us," my friend said, motioning to a gentleman at the other end of the community table.

I awkwardly glanced over to see an inconspicuous older gentleman in a fishing hat sipping his coffee and reading a copy of *The Tampa Tribune*.

"I think he's listening to our conversation," my friend continued, suggesting that we end our conversation and move our meeting somewhere more private.

I couldn't believe what I was witnessing. I felt like one of the friends of John Nash in the movie *A Beautiful Mind*, dreadfully concerned that my friend was losing it. And all over a pretty bad idea. We left Starbucks and I never heard my friend mention the idea again. I was relieved. The 20 minutes I spent with him confirmed that he wasn't the right guy to start that company.

While most entrepreneurs aren't nearly as dramatic as my friend, I see elements of this behavior all the time. Startups are a lot like babies. The moment an infant is born you fall madly in love with it. You're naturally protective of it, keeping it at home in a bubble that will ensure it doesn't interact with any outside forces. But eventually, you know it's best for your baby to get out into the world to interact with other babies, people, and experiences. These interactions build the baby's immune system and make it stronger. Ideas are similar except they don't need to stay inside the home nearly as long as babies do. Once you have a good grasp on what your idea is, find people in your network who have experience and expertise that will make your idea stronger. Talk openly with these people about your idea without fear of legal repercussions. The more you air out your idea, exposing it to people different from you, the stronger it will get and the quicker you will learn whether or not it's an idea worth pursuing.

The next time you are hesitant about sitting down at a coffee shop with a friend or acquaintance to talk about your idea, consider this: What are the chances that the person sitting at the table next to you will hear your idea, think it's as great as you do, have the expertise and drive to build the idea into a business, and will be able to do it all better than you can? If you think the chances are high, then you're not the right person to build that business. The benefits of vetting your idea in broad daylight far outweigh the risks. Remember, ideas are cheap. Talk freely about them. If you have the right idea and the right experience to build it into a business, no one will be able to stop you.

Chapter 4: Start with stories

When Tony first pitched me on Citizinvestor, he came to the table with a great idea but no clue as to how to bring it to launch. I am constantly being asked for advice from similar first-time entrepreneurs who think they are sitting on a golden egg of an idea, but have no idea how to hatch it. One of the reasons I wrote this book is to share my advice with more people to help them quickly get their ideas out of their heads, onto paper, and into the real world as tangible products, companies, nonprofits, etc.

If you have an idea for a startup but have no clue where to start, I will give you the same advice I gave Tony at our first meeting about Citizinvestor: Start with stories. I've found that the most common reason people get stuck in the "idea stage" is that they haven't clearly defined *what* their idea is and *how* they envision their solution working. When people ask me what they should do first to bring their idea to launch, I think they expect me to advise them to find a web developer, choose a name for the company, or draw out on a napkin how their product will work. Nope! In my opinion, none of these are the best starting points. Start by telling a story of how your product will work.

Let me show you what I mean by sharing a "user story" Tony drafted following our first meeting. I tasked Tony with writing a story of how a citizen would use Citizinvestor to donate to a civic project. A huge *Game of Thrones* fan, Tony had some fun with the exercise:

> Arya Stark is a citizen of the City of King's Landing. She is frustrated because there isn't any

place in the city for her to practice her swords with her dancing master, Syrio Forel. She goes to her local civic association meeting to complain. Once there, Arya is told by the president of the civic association, Renly Baratheon, that the City had thought it was a good idea to build a new park in the city, but they did not have any money in the budget because all the money had been allocated to the Tourney of the Hand. However, the City of King's Landing had agreed to put the project on Citizinvestor.com and if the goal of $100,000 was met, the park would be built.

Arya is very excited and runs home to contribute to the project. She types in the address for Citizinvestor.com and is taken to the homepage. On the homepage she sees an explanation of Citizinvestor, a sampling of projects in different cities, and an area that allows her to search projects.

Arya types in "King's Landing" (her city's name) and "Park" (the type of project she is looking to fund). Two projects pop up: a small park on the north side of the city, and a large park on the south side of the city. Next to the projects is a brief narrative description of the project (with a "read more" tab if additional reading is desired) and some quick metrics (goal, deadline, currently pledged).

Arya clicks on the north-side project and is taken to a new page that is exclusively dedicated to that project. There is a large "Invest Now" button on this page with a blank area to the left where users can put in the amount they wish to fund. Arya types in $250 and clicks the "Invest Now" button. A message pops up telling her she needs to sign up for a free account in order to donate.

Arya goes to sign up, where she provides her name, address, credit card information, email address, username, and password. After she clicks "submit" she gets a page that thanks her for signing up, tells her an email has been sent to her, and gives an explanation of how the credit card information is used and how crowdfunding works. There is a button that says "go back to project." Once back on the project page, Arya retypes in her amount of $250, and clicks the "Invest Now" button. She is taken to a new page which has her amount listed, with the last four digits of her credit card and her address listed for her to confirm. On this page, there are also opt-in check-boxes where she can be alerted at various points in a project's lifecycle (when the project is fully funded, when it is 90% funded, when the deadline is one week away, etc.). Arya verifies the information, clicks the opt-in check-boxes, and clicks "submit." She is taken to a page that thanks her for donating and states that an email has been sent confirming the contribution and (maybe) re-explaining the crowdfunding process.

Until writing this, Citizinvestor was an amorphous

idea in Tony's head. Writing out this user story allowed Tony to crystallize the idea by thinking through:

- The problem Citizinvestor would solve
- How a user might find out about Citizinvestor
- How a user would find a project they wanted to donate to
- Various features the product would need (project categories, the ability to search for projects by city, etc.)
- How users would donate to projects

Tony's user story was far from perfect and it would go through many iterations before we started any other work on Citizinvestor; but it was an excellent place to start. To this day, Tony credits this exercise as the most helpful tool in clarifying what Citizinvestor would be. It's easy to explain an idea without real (or fantasy) names, problems, and clicks of the mouse. Explaining your idea in narrative form will show you where the holes are in your idea, allowing you to plug them with words rather than code.

Coming up with a great idea is easy. Executing a great idea is hard. But here's the good news: anyone can tell a story, so start there. Get out your pen and paper (or, as I prefer, a Google Doc) and start the process of bringing your idea to life!

Chapter 5: Stay focused on what matters most

The start of any startup is intoxicating. For us at Citizinvestor, it seemed like we were on a rocket ship barreling towards the moon.

Tony and I first met about Citizinvestor on April 5, 2012. By 10:00 that evening, we had already put together a preliminary analysis of the competitive landscape and decided on a business model: We would take 5% of all projects that were successfully funded by citizens. By April 14, we had decided on the name of the company and purchased the domain name citizinvestor.com. Four days later, over a beer in Washington, D.C., I sealed the deal to bring our third and final Co-founder onto the team: Erik Rapprich. A master in web production management, Erik walked me through his plan for getting citizinvestor.com to launch as soon as possible. With the plan in place, we were off and running!

Nothing is more fun than building a web product from scratch. The weeks we spent building Citizinvestor were among the most fun to date. By May 4, we had our first round of wireframes (essentially visual blueprints of the site) completed and the scope of version one of the product locked down.

An early wireframe of what would become the Citizinvestor project page

Knowing that it would take some time to lock down our first customer, we decided to start blogging about how Citizinvestor would work once we launched. The strategy behind this was twofold. First, we wanted to stick our flag in the ground as one of the first companies crowdfunding government projects; and second, we thought that if we started talking about Citizinvestor publicly, we might be able to generate buzz in the press about our project. Announcing what we were working on accomplished both goals, but we significantly underestimated the wave of hype we were about to generate.

Before we even launched Citizinvestor, we had been glowingly profiled in seven publications and asked to deliver a TEDx talk. We then found out that we had been chosen from 200 applicants as a finalist for Code for America's inaugural startup accelerator program. The icing on the cake came at a moment when I had one foot in my new venture as a civic entrepreneur, and another in my former life as a political operative.

It was the last week of August 2012, and I was spending most of my time at the Republican National Convention being hosted in my hometown of Tampa, Florida. I was walking to a briefing by the Romney campaign's Digital Director when I received an email informing me that Citizinvestor had been selected to receive a $5,000 grant at an event hosted by Rock the Vote and a new group called StartUp RockOn. I couldn't believe it. We didn't have a product or a single customer yet, and here someone was just going to hand over $5,000 because they thought our idea was cool.

We were asked to pick up the check at a club in Ybor City that night. Rock the Vote was hosting a party with DJ Steve Aoki, or as Tony kept calling him, "DJ Okie Dokie." Now, as I've already established, Tony and I both live lives that don't fit the traditional startup founder mold. We prefer Brooks Brothers to Urban Outfitters, coffee to Red Bull, and reading a book at home to pub crawls. Going to a club in infamous Ybor

City was not a common occurrence for us. And by not a common occurrence, I of course mean that we had never been to one before. But hey, someone was giving us free money, and boy did we need it.

That same night, my wife and I had tickets to the opening of the Republican National Convention, but I figured we could make it to the party to pick up the check and still have time to get back to the Convention Center to hear Ann Romney and Chris Christie speak. As we walked into the club, we couldn't have stuck out more if we tried. Tony, Kara, and I stepped out of a Brooks Brothers catalog onto an alcohol-laden dance floor crammed with glow stick waving teenagers in what can only loosely be described as clothes. Eric Wilson, a good friend and former colleague of mine, went as far as to sport a bow tie and a handful of placards touting the record of his client, House Speaker John Boehner.

Eric after losing the bow tie

The club thumping (kids still say that, right?), we awkwardly made our way upstairs to collect our $5,000 check. We were enthusiastically greeted by the event's organizers who heaped praise after praise on Citizinvestor. With the launch of the site imminent, everyone around us was setting expectations at a level matched only by the volume of DJ Okie Dokie and his screaming fans. We couldn't help but mistake the hype for success.

While press, speaking engagements, and events that promoted Citizinvestor were great, they weren't what mattered most to our core business. About a year after we launched Citizinvestor, Tony and I were feeling overwhelmed by the number of things we were working on, so we took the time to clearly define what mattered most to building our startup into a sustainable business. We were able to boil it down to two things: getting municipal governments to post crowdfunding projects, and getting those projects funded. Those were the only two things that made us money and moved us toward sustainability. With those two things clearly defined, we held a number of "stop doing" meetings where we looked at every task we had on our to-do lists and asked ourselves whether or not it helped us get projects or get them funded. If the answer was no, we dropped the task without hesitation. In our first "stop doing" meeting, we dropped half of the things we were working on and the company was much better for it.

At the start of a startup you have no map. You are charting uncharted territory. When you're in that position, it's easy to trick yourself into believing that the things that are the most fun are the things that are helping you build your business. And maybe they are!

But in our experience, the things that matter the most are the things that are the hardest and least fun to do. After you have come down from the intoxicating launch of your startup, get focused on what matters most as quickly as possible.

Chapter 6: Be comfortable in your own skin

I have been a Chick-fil-A fanatic for as long as I can remember. Not only do I love Chick-fil-A's food (a Spicy Chicken Sandwich meal with a Diet Coke and Chick-fil-A sauce is my go-to, in case you're wondering), but I also love the company's leadership, principles, and business acumen. When my first startup was "acquihired" in 2011 by Engage, my new bosses asked me, "If you could consult with any organization in the world, which would it be?" It took me less than two seconds to provide my answer: Chick-fil-A. After a few weeks of strategizing the best way in the door of my dream client, I secured a meeting with the head of Chick-fil-A's digital marketing team to pitch one of our products. I was ecstatic! Now, the tough part began.

I worked on the pitch to Chick-fil-A with my new boss and a Founding Partner at Engage, Patrick Ruffini. As we were putting together a slide about our experience, we started to question how much we wanted to emphasize our almost completely political backgrounds. After all, we were going to be pitching a company that sold chicken sandwiches. Why would they care about our political experience?

But we were proud of our political backgrounds, and even if we weren't, they were impossible to hide. Patrick had risen to a good degree of fame in national Republican circles that widely viewed him as one of the leading pioneers of "digital politics" on the right side of the political aisle. Patrick had served as the Webmaster for the Bush-Cheney campaign in 2004, and then led digital strategy at the Republican National Committee in 2006. Engage's other Partner, Mindy Finn, earned her stripes leading digital strategy for the Romney campaign in 2008. My background up until this point was also heavily political. My first startup, Direct Media Strategies, consulted mostly with conservative political campaigns and causes on how to use the Internet to win elections. Nearly every professional experience I had before that was political too, including managing an online political news organization and an internship in The White House.

In the age of Google, there is no hiding who we are. So we decided to double down on our experience, and craft a narrative about why our experience would be valuable to Chick-fil-A. Sitting around a conference table at Engage's offices in Washington, D.C., Mindy brilliantly articulated how to connect our political experience to the corporate world. Mindy argued that every political campaign and brand wants to do three things:

1. Identify a group of potential voters/customers
2. Engage those individuals with the candidate/brand
3. Activate those individuals to vote/buy a product

The pitch to Chick-fil-A, largely structured around these parallels, was the best I've ever been a part of. Our contact made clear that Chick-fil-A valued the experience we brought winning votes and understood the parallels to selling chicken. We had doubled down on our backgrounds and it paid off in a big way. Patrick and I had a hard time tamping down our giddiness as we walked out the door of Chick-fil-A HQ.

At Citizinvestor, this idea of being comfortable in

our own skin has manifested itself in a number of ways. One of the first pitches Tony and I ever gave was to the notoriously liberal City of Portland. Hovering over my iPhone, Tony and I were taken aback by how the blunt conversation began.

"So, we Googled you guys before the call," our contacts in the Mayor's office said.

Long pause.

"Aaaand you guys are political operatives," they concluded, leaving us unsure as to whether it was a statement or a question.

"Yup. Well, *former* political operatives," I replied.

"Cool."

Silence.

"And Republicans?" they replied, this time clearly asking a question.

"Yup!" Tony shot back.

"OK, cool. So, will you guys screen projects the City posts to Citizinvestor? Like, will you take a project down if we want to raise money to fund a needle exchange program?"

Out of the thousands of questions government entities have asked us at Citizinvestor, none have topped that one. For the record, we never screen projects posted by government entities on Citizinvestor. The City of Portland has yet to post a project to crowdfund a needle exchange program. Being Republicans, we initially thought that we would be black sheep working with cities with predominantly Democratic leadership. But that has never appeared to be a problem for us. In fact, by not "hiding the ball" about our backgrounds, I believe it has made our political affiliation a nonissue.

In some cases, being comfortable in our own skin has even won us fans, as in the case of tech mogul Tim O'Reilly. While in San Francisco a week before our first attempted launch of Citizinvestor (see the next chapter), Tony and I had the great privilege of meeting with Tim to get his feedback on what we were working on. Sitting in a conference room at Code for America's offices, I launched right into my pitch, sharing with Tim the unapologetic political backgrounds of each founder. A naturally fast talker, I zipped right through the "Team" slide of our pitch deck and began talking through the "Market" section when Tim interrupted me to say, "You know what I love about you guys? You're Republicans!" His tone allowed us to translate the comment to, "I love that you guys aren't hiding who you are." It was a lesson we haven't forgotten.

In a startup, you are constantly asking people for something. You are asking potential customers to buy your product. You are asking investors to gamble a sizable fortune on your idea. You are asking reporters to cover news about your company. When you're constantly asking for things critical to your company's survival, it's easy to pull chameleon-like metamorphoses to close deals. Resist the temptation. It takes one Google search to reveal the true you, so don't hide from it. Find creative ways to use your background and experience to your advantage.

Chapter 7: Be flexible

"Sleep tight" are two words that, on any other night, would have seemed creepy to hear from our developer. But at 11:44 p.m. on August 20, 2012, it was exactly what I needed to hear in order to rest easy. I had emailed Mathias Hansen, our Lead Developer on Citizinvestor, to let him know that I was hitting the sack. Mathias, Erik, and Nick Walters (our Lead Designer) were pulling the all-nighter necessary to launch Citizinvestor to the world and, in my imagination, someday turn our story into an Aaron Sorkin movie.

"Everything is running smooth so far," Mathias emailed me as the team was transitioning the site from its development environment to its permanent home at Citizinvestor.com. I had been checking my email incessantly, looking for reassurance that when I woke up the following morning, our startup would be officially launched. Most people wouldn't be able to sleep on the eve of such a monumental occasion. Not me. All of our ducks were in a row. The site was in great shape. We had two amazing cities with projects on the site. Top-tier media had stories ready to publish about our launch. I was ready to sleep like a baby. By the time my head hit the pillow at 11:45 p.m., I was already halfway to REM.

I felt great as I sprang out of bed the next morning. And then, like a land mine in an otherwise beautiful field of emails, our plans blew to pieces. The subject line in the email from Mathias said it all: "URGENT! Amazon Payments problems."

I immediately knew we were screwed.

Mathias' email went on: "I regret to inform you all that because of unforeseen circumstances we are currently not able to accept any payments. After switching everything to production and testing all the features, we got a show-stopper when trying to invest in projects."

Mathias, recently immigrated from Denmark, carried a thick accent; but his English was good enough to colloquially articulate what a "payments problem" meant for our startup. It was a "show-stopper" of the greatest magnitude, one that threatened to close the curtain before our show ever began.

Now, let's backtrack for a moment. Here we were, set to launch a crowdfunding platform for government projects. The *only* feature that mattered was the ability for citizens to donate to projects. If that was broken, the whole business was broken. Following Kickstarter's proven payments system, we had decided to use Amazon Payments to process donations to projects. But when we went to take Citizinvestor.com live, our developers were notified that Amazon had to manually approve Citizinvestor to accept payments. The worst part was that even though this error was caught at 1:41 a.m. Eastern Standard Time, we had to wait until Amazon's phones opened at 10:00 a.m. to resolve the issue. One thing was clear: We weren't launching Citizinvestor today.

The payments problem turned out to be a domino that sent others falling fast. While Mathias and Erik worked with Amazon, Tony and I immediately focused our attention on keeping our first two customers, the cities of Chicago and Boston, from jumping ship. When we started pitching Citizinvestor, we imagined it would be tough to find a city willing to be the guinea pig for our experiment. We would have been thrilled to get any cities as our first customers, but the market-mover cities of Chicago and Boston were a dream come true. But that dream quickly turned into a nightmare. The nonprofit the City of Boston had chosen to partner with on their first Citizinvestor project got cold feet the minute we notified them of the problem with Amazon. Just like that, Boston was overboard. This was an especially embarrassing problem as we had embargoed a story to Mashable.com with a quote from Boston Mayor Thomas Menino that we then had to pull back.

To add to our problems, Boston pulling out left us with just one city for launch. The plan all along had been to launch Citizinvestor with projects in multiple cities to symbolize to investors and news media one of the pillars of our business strategy. We believed that by focusing on getting as many municipal governments to post as many projects as quickly as possible, we would have a strong first-mover advantage in the market. Government entities tend to "follow the leader" into uncharted territory. We believed that if we could clearly demonstrate that more municipalities were choosing Citizinvestor over our competitors, we could win the market and hold onto market share by successfully funding projects (a strategy that would eventually prove true). Launching with just one city would make it harder for us to make that case.

While we were debating internally whether or not to be flexible in our launch strategy and go live with "just Chicago," the Chicago Teachers Union made our decision for us. On August 29, the Teachers Union declared its intent to strike, making some of the largest political waves of the summer. Way downstream, the ripples of this decision capsized our plans for launch as the City informed us that the project they had posted on Citizinvestor to provide school supplies to 1,000 students in need had to be yanked. When I got the call from our contact in Chicago, I backed myself into the corner of my office and slowly slid to the floor as if sinking to the bottom of the ocean.

The flexibility and resolve of our team in the two weeks following our failure to launch is one of the moments I am most proud of during our time working on Citizinvestor thus far. Instead of sulking around and looking for people to blame, everyone put aside their pride and calmly thought outside the box of our once seemingly flawless plans. Three days after our Amazon snafu, our team had replaced Amazon Payments with WePay – the payments provider we still partner with today. On the sales side, Tony and I caved on our plans to launch in multiple cities and soon locked down an equally incredible first partner in the City of Philadelphia. We rebuilt the product and much of the company in just three weeks, and on September 12, 2012, our launch went off without a hitch.

Citizinvestor is not the only startup with a horror story like this one. If you're launching a new product, some of your plans will get destroyed. It's inevitable. In those moments of crisis, the best way out is to stay humble, be flexible, and surround yourself with people who will do the same.

PART TWO
Grinding

Bet the farm
If they don't tell you yes, they are telling you no
If it seems too good to be true, it is
Raise money from friends and family with caution
Startups are emotional roller coasters
Startups are a young person's game

Chapter 8: Bet the farm

Most startups are faced with a do-or-die moment early in their lifetime – a moment when the founders are forced to bet the farm. For us, that moment came just months after launch.

There was a lot of hype surrounding the launch of Citizinvestor. The City of Philadelphia had agreed to be the guinea pig for our grand experiment, posting the first crowdfunding project to Citizinvestor. At the time, this made Philadelphia the largest city in the United States to ever crowdfund a government project. The response to the launch of the project and our company was overwhelmingly positive. *Fast Company* summed up our hopes and dreams by saying that "crowdfunding could have as much impact in the public sector as it's having on the private side."

It was one thing to get a city like Philadelphia to post a project to Citizinvestor; it was a whole other thing to answer the ultimate question facing our young startup: Would citizens donate money to government projects? When it became clear to us that the answer for our first and widely publicized project in Philadelphia was a resounding "no," we knew our next project would make or break our startup.

Thankfully, the City of Boston had posted their first project just weeks after our launch (and, most importantly, before the Philadelphia project failed). The City of Boston wanted to raise $6,480 to provide iPads and Bluetooth technology to 10 visually impaired students and train them on how to use these tools. The project seemed perfect! How could we *not* get citizens to donate money to provide blind students with this amazing technology? But raising the funds proved far more difficult than we expected.

With our focus initially split between the Philadelphia and Boston projects, the crowdfunding campaign in Boston started slow. This being just our second project, we were experimenting with everything we could think of to help drive donations. We tried to reach mothers of blind children by targeting Facebook ads to women in Boston, over the age of 30, who liked the Facebook pages of national organizations for blind people; we emailed 177 optometry professors and students in the Greater Boston area; we emailed organizations that represented the visually impaired in Boston. Some of this was working, but most of it was not.

Halfway through the Boston project's funding cycle, the Philadelphia project officially failed, having only raised $1,694 of its $12,875 goal before the deadline. Making matters worse, we had little reason to believe that the Boston project would succeed. If we went 0/2, we knew we were through. Sales to other cities would dry up and the press that lauded the promise of our new venture would quickly point to our failed experiment. We were running out of ideas, and more critically, we were running out of time.

In an act of desperation, I suggested to Tony that I hop on a flight to Boston and spend a week pounding the pavement to try to get the project funded. Having no better ideas, I booked a plane ticket and three nights in a B&B. Total cost? $739.30 – roughly one-fifth of what we had in the bank after we cashed the check from our event with DJ Okie Dokie. When I booked the ticket, we had no plan for what I would do when I actually got to Boston, but that didn't matter. We had to do whatever it took to save our startup.

In the week or so before I departed for Boston, we had our rock-star intern (and moonlighting DJ), Dave Wistocki, build a map of every optometrist and eyeglass shop in downtown Boston. Dave put together a walking/subway route for me so that when I landed at Boston Logan Airport, I could literally hit the ground running, popping into the shops of eye doctors, begging them to donate to our project to help visually impaired students in Boston. In retrospect, the whole pitch sounded a lot like a SPAM email from a Nigerian prince. And it was totally ineffective.

After two days of me playing traveling salesman, we hadn't seen a single donation come in. So I spent the remainder of my time doing the one thing we knew was driving donations to projects: press. I quickly scheduled interviews with *The Boston Globe* and Boston's *NPR* affiliate, *WBUR*. In the days following the interviews, a number of donations came in from boston.com and Google searches during the radio interview. But the donation amounts were small, and we were still nowhere near reaching our goal.

As I boarded the plane to fly back to Tampa, I felt deflated, assured that our experiment would soon be over. I couldn't help but see the cheesy parallel between what we were experiencing and what I witnessed just two nights earlier at the Romney campaign's victory-turned-pity party in Boston – two organizations with lots of hope and hype crashing as quickly as they arose.

Once back in Tampa, Tony and I regrouped, still intent on going all in with our Boston project. But how? We had tried everything we could think of.

"What if we donated Citizinvestor money to get the project within striking distance of its goal?" Tony asked me.

It was a bold "bet the farm" move for a startup that had a little more than $4,000 in the bank. But it was our best option by far. We donated $1,250 to the project from Citizinvestor, Inc., and in the next nine days, 11 of the project's 47 donations rolled in. We had our first successfully funded project.

Was flying to our partner city and donating money from the company sustainable for Citizinvestor? Of course not. But it didn't matter. We just needed to survive another day, and by betting the farm, we did.

Chapter 9: If they don't tell you yes, they are telling you no

As Tony began talking through the "Revenue Projections" slide of our pitch deck, I sat back in my chair amazed at how well the meeting was going. Based on the reaction of the investor we were meeting with, you would have thought we had made this pitch hundreds of times. Everything she said made us believe that we would soon be receiving a check for the $250,000 we were requesting to finance Citizinvestor. Her words echoed what everyone familiar with raising venture capital had told us on this trip to San Francisco:

> "I really love what you guys are doing."

> "This makes a lot of sense."

> "You guys are solving a very real problem."

> "This has the potential to be a huge market."

> "Our fund is really interested in this new market."

We had heard these things so many times in the four days we spent in Silicon Valley, that we were forced to believe they were true. As we walked out of the meeting, we exuded confidence heading into our last investor pitch of the trip. But there was no time to gloat. We only had 45 minutes to get to our final meeting which, per the request of the investor we were meeting, would take place at my favorite spot in all of San Francisco: Mario's

Bohemian Cigar Store Cafe. We had planned on taking an Uber taxi to the meeting, but the San Francisco sun was making a rare appearance, so I suggested that we walk. According to Google Maps, it would only take us 15 minutes to reach our destination by foot. "Easy," I thought. "We have plenty of time."

It wasn't long after we started our trek that my iPhone led us to a massive staircase. I checked Google Maps. Sure enough, we were heading in the right direction. "One giant staircase can't be that bad," I thought to myself, weighing the cost/benefit analysis of retreating back to the road to find a taxi versus ascending Telegraph Hill in our suits and laptop bags. As we reached the top of the staircase, we quickly realized this was just the first in a series of uphill climbs to get to our final meeting. Our pride intact, Tony and I doubled down on our choice of transportation and continued up the arduous path. We used the time to debrief from the meeting we had just wrapped up.

"That went really well," Tony said. "I think they could be our lead investor in this round of funding."

We were in agreement. "Absolutely," I replied, keeping my answers brief in order to preserve oxygen for our hike up San Francisco's Mount Everest.

"I'm surprised at how quickly everyone is buying our vision for how large this market can be," Tony continued. "I thought we were going to have to spend a lot more time selling that."

"Yeah," I replied. "I'm shocked at how easy that has been."

After a seemingly endless climb/walk, our destination was in sight. As we approached Mario's Bohemian Cigar Store Cafe, I opened my email and found that our contact had provided instructions on where to meet. "Outside table if weather is nice...that corner table if it isn't," his email read. Standing awkwardly around the corner from the cafe, Tony and I quickly debated whether or not the "weather [was] nice," hoping that the investor didn't walk by and hear our conversation. Coming from Tampa, Florida, it's hard to tell what San Franciscans consider to be nice weather. It seemed nice enough to us, so we grabbed a table caddy-corner to beautiful Washington Square Park. To ensure I didn't miss him, I frantically Googled pictures of our contact. His picture creepily in hand, I was on the lookout. A few minutes rolled by and there was no sign of him. After another few minutes, Tony suggested that I check the corner table inside the cafe. Sure enough, there he was. I motioned through the window for Tony to join us, and he frantically scrambled to bring our laptops and lattes inside. We obviously didn't see eye to eye with this guy on the weather, but that was OK so long as we saw eye to eye on our vision for Citizinvestor.

    The meeting was already off to an awkward start. It only got worse when Tony pulled out the laptop with our pitch deck and then, after realizing how small the coffee table was, awkwardly shoved it back into his bag. Just minutes into our now nearly memorized pitch, the investor started pelting us with questions. It took less than 15 minutes for him to tell us that although he liked what we were doing, he didn't think Citizinvestor was an investable business yet, so he was out as a potential investor.

    "You win some, you lose some," I thought to myself, recalling all of the meetings we had with other investors that week that we thought went great.

"How have your meetings with other investors gone?" he asked us.

Tony jumped in. "They've been going great! Everyone seems really interested in what we are doing and they've expressed interest in investing once we get a few crowdfunding projects successfully funded."

The investor had finished his latte and our scheduled time was almost up. Even though he wasn't interested in investing in Citizinvestor, he was kind enough to offer us numerous nuggets of advice. But the only piece of advice that has stuck with us was what he said next: "If they don't tell you yes, they are telling you no."

After he left, Tony and I talked through the meeting. We loved the investor's honesty, but we didn't believe that "maybe" actually meant "no" with other investors. We *couldn't* believe it after all of the other great meetings we had that week. But hindsight is 20/20, and the reason we remember this piece of advice is because it is absolutely true. The investor that gave us the confidence to climb San Francisco Everest never wrote us a check. In fact, we still haven't raised a dime of capital from the dozens of investors we met on that trip that told us everything we wanted to hear, except for "Yes!" In a startup, everyone will tell you that you and your company are great. Their encouragement will make the path to victory seem easy. It's not. Nothing worth doing ever is. If they don't tell you yes, they are telling you no.

Achy and hungry, Tony and I stayed behind to finish our lattes and order food. Much like raising capital, our walk to the meeting which initially seemed like a piece of cake had quickly turned into an extreme adventure sport. The metaphor was completely lost on us in the moment.

Chapter 10: If it seems too good to be true, it is

While we were in survival mode at Citizinvestor, every member of the team was drawing income from something other than our new project. When I made the leap from Engage to focus more on Citizinvestor, I consulted with a few companies in order to pay the bills. One of my clients was another technology startup that was looking to raise capital. One day, the CEO of this startup called me about a game-changing meeting he had with a potential investor. To protect the innocent, we will call this investor "the Wizard of Oz." This code name will seem apt once you get to the end of this story.

"Jordan, I just got done meeting with the Wizard," my client told me.

"Who?" I asked.

"You don't know who the Wizard is!?" he shot back, shocked at my ignorance.

"Nope," I said. "Never heard of him."

As my client walked me through this mysterious figure's impressive résumé, I frantically googled his name, sure I would find a robust Wikipedia page, profiles in *The Wall Street Journal*, and his name on the *Forbes* 500 list. Nothing. Then, my client dropped a bombshell: "Jordan, they've raised a billion-dollar fund here in Florida to invest in early-stage startups."

Now, I don't claim to be an expert on raising venture capital, but this seemed preposterous even on the surface. An early-stage venture capital fund of this size would be one of the largest in the country. And they were setting up shop in Florida instead of Silicon

Valley!? No offense, home state, but this seemed absurd. My client assured me the whole thing was legit. He also said that the investors wanted to meet the rest of the team and myself in just a few days. Feeling like the Tin Man skipping down the yellow brick road in lockstep with Dorothy and friends, I couldn't wait to see if the Wizard lived up to the hype.

As I was driving to the meeting, my client called to share an important piece of intel: One of the Wizard's minions informed him that the investors would be making him an offer…today.

"That's insane," I told him. "They know next to nothing about the company."

"He said the offer would be seven figures," my client replied, his tone communicating a tinge of disbelief.

When I heard "seven figures" I almost swerved off the interstate. Here was a company that didn't have a product or a single customer and they were about to be offered *at least* $1,000,000. Meanwhile, Citizinvestor had a great product, amazing customers, yet virtually zero interest from investors.

"That's incredible," I told my client, quickly swapping the words "asinine" and "incredible" in my mental dictionary.

I met my client and two members of his team in a parking lot just outside the Wizard's palace. The shady lot was the first sign that this was no Emerald City. As the four of us walked along the red brick road towards the office, we took bets on what the offer would be. "I bet they give us $1,000,000 for 50% of the company," the CEO said.

"A $2,000,000 valuation for this company seems too good to be true," I thought. But as we sat down at the table with the investors, what I thought no longer mattered. I was there to sit back and listen.

The CEO started out on his pitch to the investors. About 15 minutes in, the Wizard interrupted. "How much do you guys need?" he asked.

Taken aback by the suddenness of the question, my client fumbled for an answer.

"$2,000,000?" the Wizard prodded.

"Umm," my client mumbled in disbelief, still unable to spit out words.

"OK, let's do this. How about we give you $3,000,000 for 30% of the company? Will that work for you guys?"

It took straining every muscle in my face to keep my jaw from hitting the floor. Thankfully, my client gave me an out when he asked the Wizard if his team could step outside for a minute to discuss the offer. As soon as Dorothy, the Scarecrow, the Lion, and myself got out the door, we giggled like schoolgirls.

"They just valued the company at $10,000,000," my client said. "This makes me a paper millionaire," another member of his team said in disbelief. We weren't in the hallway long. When we walked back in the room, my client accepted the offer on the spot.

"Great! We will send over some paperwork for you to look at and we'll go from there," the Wizard said, obviously quite pleased. As the meeting wrapped up, my client mentioned to the Wizard that I had a startup called Citizinvestor that was currently raising capital. "Send me that deal," the Wizard implored.

Ten days later, I was back to try to see lightning strike twice, this time for Citizinvestor. Tony and I were skeptical that this investment outfit was legit, but we figured it couldn't hurt to meet. Always punctual, Tony and I showed up at 9:25 a.m. – five minutes before the meeting's scheduled start time. It wasn't until 9:45 that someone showed up. It was the Wizard himself. After realizing he didn't have a key, he called one of his associates to see why he was late. Although we could only hear one side of the conversation, it was obvious that the guy on the other line had just rolled out of bed. Tony looked at me as if to ask, "Who are these people?"

Our pitch started more than 30 minutes late, but it only took five minutes for the Wizard to interrupt us to say that our whole business model was flawed. Midway through his rant, the Wizard looked at Tony and said, "Tony, you're looking at me like I'm an idiot." Tony quickly denied the charge, but we both knew that's *exactly* what he was thinking.

Once we had a look at the paperwork for the proposed deal, it was clear the Wizard's fund was a facade. There was no billion-dollar fund. In fact, the investors used the networks of the startup founders they were recruiting to help build their fund. My gut was right all along, but unfortunately for my client, they wasted a lot of time chasing the deal.

If a deal seems too good to be true, it is. Ask as many questions as you can on the front end to save yourself time, money, and focus.

Chapter 11: Raise money from friends and family with caution

There's a dirty little secret about raising startup capital that is rarely shared. As a first- and sometimes even second-time entrepreneur, you are probably going to raise your first round of capital from friends and family. That's exactly what we did at Citizinvestor after months of false hope from institutional investors and borderline Ponzi schemes (see previous chapter). We were fortunate enough to have wealthy friends and family who could afford to take a gamble on us as founders.

According to research published by "business crowdfunding platform" Fundable in December 2013, there are 6,780,000 startups launched in the United States each year (remember this the next time you say you have no competition). These ~6.8 million startups raise $531 billion in capital per year, $60 billion of which comes from friends and family – the second highest source of capital behind only the founders' personal savings and credit. According to the report, 38% of startups raise capital from friends and family, and while the research does not breakdown the percentage of startups with first-time founders who raise capital from friends and family, it's almost certainly higher. Here's why.

Most investors do not invest in ideas. They invest in teams, and more specifically, the founders of the company. The chance that your idea in its original state is going to be a monstrous success is infinitesimally slim. Good investors know that. But great entrepreneurs are intuitive and self-aware enough to know when to pivot their ideas away from their original plans and towards the greatest opportunities. As a first-time entrepreneur, it's tough to convince an unknown investor to trust that you are the kind of founder that can navigate a startup through those turbulent first months or years. Your friends and family on the other hand know you. They know your character, your intuition, and your drive, and they're much more willing to bet big on you. But make no mistake about it, they are betting on you, not your idea.

Raising capital from anyone – friends and family, angel investors, venture capitalists, etc. – should always be Plan Z. When you take on investors, you give up some control of your company and your vision. Raising money from friends and family adds another awkward dimension to the mix and has the potential to add a significant amount of pressure and strain to your relationship. Hold out on raising capital as long as you can. If you are single and have no kids, work on your startup at night when you come home from your day job. Focus on getting paying customers as quickly as possible in order to fund your venture to the point where you can take the leap and work on it full-time. The lessons you learn when working for sweat equity are priceless. Bootstrap your startup as long as you can, but when you can't bootstrap any longer and you're considering raising capital from friends and family, here are a few tips to keep in mind.

- **Explain the risk in detail.** You would never start a cold pitch to a venture capitalist outlining the risks of your new company. But that's exactly what you should do with friends and family, especially if they are not experienced investors.

The vast majority of startups fail. The odds suggest that yours will too. Your friends and family will want to believe that your startup is the exception, which is why you need to stress the risks of your venture on the front end.

- **Only raise money from those who can afford to lose it all.** Sorry to harp on risk, but I'm trying to help you avoid awkward Christmas dinners for the next 20 years. Just because a friend or family member offers you an investment, doesn't mean you have to take it. Only accept an investment from those in your network who can afford to lose it all. Friends and family investments should be a small portion of their liquid wealth. Don't ask them to take a second mortgage out on their house.
- **Keep the deal structure simple.** The seed money we raised for Citizinvestor was structured as a simple convertible note – a common deal structure for raising money from friends and family. A convertible note is a type of loan that the holder can convert into a specified number of shares of stock in the startup or cash of equal value. One of the benefits of convertible note deals is how quick and easy they are to execute. You want as little legal back-and-forth with friends and family as possible.
- **Get a lawyer to do the paperwork.** Taking money from friends and family is dicey enough. If things go south with your startup, a poorly drafted legal document can make things really ugly. If you're raising capital from friends and family, you are doing it because your startup

desperately needs the money. But don't fall into the temptation of cutting costs by cutting a good lawyer out of the picture. Find an attorney with a wealth of experience constructing investment deals to do the paperwork right.
- **Know what you're getting into.** Taking money from friends and family requires a serious commitment to your startup. It's true that failure is not the end of the world, but failure stings much worse if you take money from those you share regular meals with and see at family birthday parties. You should never take raising capital lightly, but give the moment special respect if you decide to raise money from those you're closest to.

Raising money from friends and family has worked out great for us at Citizinvestor, and for that I feel blessed. But for every story like ours, there are hundreds of horror stories of friendships and families broken over bad investments. Startups come and go much faster than friends and family. If you have wealthy friends and family, count yourself lucky. They can be invaluable partners to helping you grow your startup. But before you ask them to invest in your company, consider the risks and make sure they do too.

Chapter 12: Startups are emotional roller coasters

The moderator of the panel asked Codecademy CEO Zach Sims what advice he could give to young people thinking about starting a company. His advice was simple, yet powerful: If you're overly emotional, don't be an entrepreneur. I had to restrain myself from shouting a hearty "amen" from the pew.

My wife will tell you that I am the emotional one in our relationship. It's always been that way. Over the years, I have learned that this is my single greatest flaw as an entrepreneur. Startups are emotional roller coasters that can violently rock you from the highest heights to the lowest lows, sometimes within just a few hours or minutes. In July of 2013, we were experiencing an especially emotional week at Citizinvestor, so I decided to journal some of the ups and downs. I have shared this journal entry below, documenting just 27 hours of the crazy ride we call Citizinvestor. Fasten your seatbelt; this is going to be exhausting.

UP

- 12:54 p.m. - The City of Evanston posts the first Citizinvestor project in the Chicago media market! The project is seeking to raise $16,200 to plant 60 trees across the city. This is a huge moment for the company marking two important milestones: the largest media market we have had a project in and potentially our largest successfully funded project to date which will help us dispel critics who say that civic crowdfunding can't scale up to larger projects.

- 12:57 p.m. - The City of Evanston informs us that they have received $1,617 in checks that they would like counted towards their project's $16,200 goal. I ask our developer, Mathias, to add these on the backend of Citizinvestor as "offline donations" as soon as possible so that the project will appear to have a lot of early momentum when citizens and City Hall employees visit the project page.
- 1:40 p.m. - Tony informs me that he is "85% sure" that the City of Orlando will post a project in the $10K-$20K range "in the next 2-3 weeks." We feel like this might be the start of the hockey stick growth we have been working towards. Or, as Tony calls it, "the BIG MO[mentum]."

DOWN
- 1:57 p.m. - Mathias informs me that he can't get the offline donations onto the Evanston project until this evening. I'm frustrated, but I understand. Citizinvestor is not Mathias' full-time job.

UP
- 2:01 p.m. - We find out that an author who has been writing about Citizinvestor for an upcoming book on civic technology wants to follow Tony and I around Las Vegas for a trip we have planned next week. To make things even more awesome, Zappos has confirmed that the author can join us for the meetings we are coordinating with Zappos and Tony Hsieh's team at the Downtown Project.

DOWN
- 4:35 p.m. - The City of San Diego informs us that they have decided to post their first crowdfunding project on Indiegogo – one of the largest crowdfunding platforms in the world. All along, our strategy has been that government entities will want to use a crowdfunding platform built just for them. This feels like a big blow to that plan.
- 6:43 a.m. - I check the Evanston project page to see if the offline donations were added last night. They weren't. I scramble to see if anyone other than Mathias can make this critical update to the project page. Jeff, a part-time developer we have just added to the team, weighs in to say that he would be happy to add the offline donations...tomorrow. Jeff lives in Japan and is heading to bed.
- 10:03 a.m. - Our partner in the City of Evanston calls Tony to inform him that, even though the project has only been on the site for less than 24 hours, people at City Hall are skittish at the project's slow start. They ask us to lower the goal to $6,480 – less than half of the original amount. Just like that, we lose a rare chance to prove we can fund larger projects. To make matters worse, it's our fault for not being able to add offline donations in a timely manner.

UP
- 10:27 a.m. - Tony informs me that he has just had a great conversation with our investor who "sees this as a movement," and is happy that we

are leading the market. When investors are happy, everyone is happy.
- 10:29 a.m. - Tony and I decide to look for our first office space in downtown Tampa as we plan to expand the team. Citizinvestor is finally starting to feel like a real company.
- 2:10 p.m. - Someone from the City of Central Falls, Rhode Island emails Tony saying they want to chat about crowdfunding projects on Citizinvestor. What makes this such a big deal is the fact that Central Falls is the only municipality in Rhode Island history to file for bankruptcy. This is a golden opportunity to tell an amazing story of how Citizinvestor can help restore broken cities.
- 4:05 p.m. - Tony sends me a message via Google Chat informing me that Butte County, California will be posting a project any day. I can't believe it! Up until now, we have been averaging one project per month. Over night, it feels like we are moving towards one per week. I chat Tony back saying, "Seriously I can not take these emotional swings anymore. not joking im going to have a heart attack."

By the grace of God, I haven't had a heart attack yet, but my grey hair has seen exponential growth since we launched Citizinvestor where the ups and downs are rivaled only by that of a stock ticker. I wish I had some practical advice for how to survive the emotional swings of a startup, but I don't. The only thing that helps me is daily reminding myself that Citizinvestor does not define me. It isn't my life purpose or my source of significance. I have more to say on this at the end of this book, but for now, just be warned that if you are an emotional person like me, startups are a wild ride.

70

Chapter 13: Startups are a young person's game

Hollywood portrays the stereotypical startup founder as an 18-22 year-old with no spouse, mortgage, kids, or plan for what to do next week. And while real life tells a *slightly* different story than this, the stereotype exists for good reason. The Citizinvestor team's experience with Silicon Valley culture has taught us a valuable lesson: Startups are a young person's game.

In October 2013, Tony and I made the decision to explore raising a second round of capital for Citizinvestor. We were growing faster than a weed and we needed to hire staff to keep up with the growth. In order to explore opening a second round of funding, we emailed everyone we knew who had connections with early-stage investors. One of the responses to these emails caught us by surprise. It was from a connection of ours who was now a partner at one of the top startup accelerator programs in Silicon Valley. Unsolicited, he asked if we "would be interested in discussing a potential fit" for their next accelerator program which was scheduled to begin in January.

We had never seriously considered applying to one of the big accelerator programs, mostly because the structure of these programs didn't fit our stage of life with wives and, for Tony, kids. Accelerator programs typically invest a small amount of capital ($25K-$50K) in your company and move your team out to Silicon Valley for three to four months where you focus intensely on supercharging the growth of your startup. They provide you with access to mentors, educational activities, and the chance to pitch a slew of investors at "demo day" which caps off the program. Tony and I knew that these accelerators provided amazing opportunities, but we suspected that they were geared to the stereotypical startup founder, *not* Tony and myself. But if we were being asked to apply, it seemed silly to not at least explore the option.

We hopped on the phone with our contact to see if their accelerator program would be a good fit for Citizinvestor. It quickly became clear that it was a good fit for both parties. We really liked and respected our contact, and he was clearly interested in the work we were doing. As we were wrapping up, we talked through the next actions of applying to the program, going through the interview process, etc., when the voice on the other end of the line told us, "I think every company we've asked to apply to the accelerator has been accepted." The message couldn't have been clearer: If we wanted it, we were in the accelerator program. But we still had to decide if that's what we wanted.

"Are we going to move our families from Tampa to San Francisco for four months?" I asked Tony after the call. The answer for Tony was a clear no. With three kids under the age of four, he was in a very different spot than I was. While I had no kids, my wife had a great job that she didn't want to walk away from. Moving away from my wife for four months was never an option, so I knew my next conversation had to be with her to gauge her interest in moving to San Francisco.

Kara and I had considered moving for jobs countless times in the past. Every single time, we felt called to stay in Tampa. Kara and I had both grown tired of the perennial conversation of whether or not to move. It was like a door that wouldn't stay shut. We would slam it shut harder each time, and it would just keep creeping open. So I was a little reticent to bring up the topic of moving for the accelerator. To my surprise, Kara was more excited about the idea than I was! She pointed out that we both love San Francisco (where we honeymooned) but we didn't want to live there. This was the perfect excuse for an "extended vacation" of sorts. As for her job, Kara had just been offered a new position and she had reason to believe she could negotiate working part-time from San Francisco. Shocked at how onboard she was with the idea, I told Tony we were in! We would move to San Francisco for the accelerator and Tony would fly out one week per month for the four-month program.

Everything was moving incredibly fast. We submitted our application for the accelerator on November 4. Our contact let us know that we would hear an answer by the end of November and that we would need to be in San Francisco the first or second week of January. Knowing how hard it can be to find a place to live in San Francisco, I immediately began looking for apartments. I had a friend who was going through the same startup accelerator at the time and was "crashing on a couch" at some stranger's apartment. This was fine four years earlier when Tony and I were crashing in a cheap New Hampshire hotel room, but my standards were a wee bit higher with Kara making the move with me.

The end of November came and went and we still hadn't heard the official word that we were accepted into the accelerator. On December 11, I followed up with our contact who was quick to respond to tell me that "we're good to go for now." Everything seemed to be going according to plan. Then, two hours later, Kara peed on a stick and everything changed. Yup! We were having our first baby.

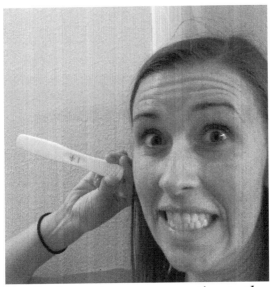

Kara perfectly captures our reaction to the news

We didn't have much time to process or celebrate the news as we were rushing out the door to meet Tony and his wife, Courtney, for dinner; but I immediately knew that this little embryo could impact our plans for moving to San Francisco. While we were told in so many words that we would be getting into the accelerator, we still didn't have a contract or a start date for the program. The uncertainty kept Kara and me from making major decisions such as whether or not Kara was going to work part-time or full-time in her new role, when we were going to tell our family and friends about the baby, etc.

Eventually, Tony and I made the decision that if the accelerator spot was offered, we would turn it down. The newest member of the Raynor family certainly factored into the decision, but the main reason was that we had just been approached about a potential acquisition and we didn't want to give up equity at the terms the accelerator was expected to offer. We never heard from our contact or anyone else at the accelerator again. We had to find out on Twitter that the program started without us. It turned out that they weren't telling us yes, and thus they were telling us no.

This whole experience confirmed what we knew all along: "Startup life" is structured around "young" founders. I put "young" in quotations because I am really referring to a stage of life rather than a specific age range. Tony and I are both relatively young in age, but not in stage of life. While we and many others have proven that it's not impossible to build a successful startup in a later stage of life, it certainly is much harder.

PART THREE

Growing

Domain knowledge matters
Take advantage of being unknown
Stay humble and accessible
Rely heavily on interns
Have the audacity to ask
Don't sell products, tell stories
Stand for something

Chapter 14: Domain knowledge matters

I come across entrepreneurs all the time who are fixated on fixing problems in industries they know nothing about. Years ago, I sat down to lunch with one such friend who was practicing law at the time. My friend shared with me how much he loathed legal work, foreshadowing a lament I would hear years later from Tony. I asked my friend what he would do if he decided to walk away from law.

"I think I want to start a startup," he said. My friend's reply caught me off guard. This was before ABC's hit show *Shark Tank* turned every American millennial into a want-to-be entrepreneur.

"Wow! That's great," I replied, not sure what to think of my friend's drastic choice of career realignment. "What's your idea?" I prodded.

"I'm not sure yet, but I think I want to build something in healthcare," he said.

The fact that my friend wanted to desert a promising legal career for a startup was surprise enough. When he told me he wanted to tackle the massive healthcare industry that he knew nothing about, I thought he was out of his mind.

One of the reasons the idea for Citizinvestor was so attractive to me was because I knew Tony had the domain expertise necessary to launch a startup in the government market. Tony spent the first years of his career practicing law, mostly with municipal and state governments as his clients. He then ran for the Tampa City Council, an experience that familiarized him with the problems citizens face when trying to get the government projects and services they want. As previously mentioned, Tony was appointed to the City of Tampa's Citizen Budget Advisory Committee after his failed bid for City Council. It was on this committee that Tony got a clear picture of the City's finances and the idea for Citizinvestor was born. Unlike many people I meet, Tony didn't sit down one day determined to think of an idea for a startup and then stumble upon Citizinvestor in some sort of light-bulb moment. Tony had a deep understanding of the problems facing local government entities, and as he spent more time thinking through those problems, the idea for Citizinvestor naturally emerged.

I joke with Tony that once he pitched me the idea for Citizinvestor his work on the project stopped and mine began. Even if he backed away from Citizinvestor today, the company would have the foundation to continue to grow largely because of the major "left/right" decisions we made early on with the aid of Tony's domain knowledge.

One such decision was to ensure that there is never a financial transaction between Citizinvestor and our government partners. Tony knew that by avoiding a direct financial transaction, we would circumvent the dreaded procurement process that makes selling to government so long and difficult. The vast majority of companies who sell to government are forced to go through procurement, and because of this bureaucratic process, it can take more than a year to close a sale. For a startup, that's way too long. Our goal has been to avoid procurement at all costs, and we have been able to do so by making two critical decisions. First, we do not charge our government partners to use Citizinvestor. This was decided early on when we ripped the model of larger crowdfunding platforms like Kickstarter and Indiegogo by simply increasing the total cost of the crowdfunded project by 5% and taking that fee once the project reached its funding goal. The second decision is the true genius of our model: We never touch the money that citizens donate to the government entity. Instead of having Citizinvestor, Inc., collect all of the money from citizens' credit cards after the project tips over the 100% threshold and then cut a check to the government entity minus our 5% fee (as some other crowdfunding platforms do), we have structured our system to where the money goes directly from citizens' credit cards into a holding account managed by WePay where the funds are then distributed to a bank account set up by the government entity.

This may sound really technical and boring, but I can't stress how huge of an advantage this has been to us selling to government entities. Almost every government entity we speak with lauds how "clean" and "simple" our model is. And you know what? As of this writing, more than 175 government entities have signed up for Citizinvestor, and we haven't had to go through procurement once. Our average "sale" (getting a municipality to post a project to the site) takes four months. These decisions we made early on have been monumental to our growth; but at the time they seemed small because Tony instinctively knew which way to turn when we encountered these forks in the road unique to the government market.

I believe in "solving problems you know" but the problems I don't know are some of the ones that most interest me. I think a lot of people share this sentiment.

Entrepreneurs are naturally curious people. We love problems we don't know the solutions to and experimenting until we find a sustainable solution. I don't think it's a mistake to tackle problems in industries you don't know, but learning the ins and outs of the problem is a critical first step before building a solution that can grow quickly. This may sound obvious, but so many entrepreneurs act like they've never heard this advice. There are two ways to gain domain knowledge. The first is to find a partner with deep knowledge of the problem you're trying to solve. This is the path my friend took to build his healthcare product by assembling a team with years of experience in the healthcare industry. If you can't find a partner with the domain expertise you're looking for, take the time to learn the problem yourself.

There's no substitute for domain knowledge and expertise. Make sure you or a partner know the ins and outs of the industry you are tackling in order to position your startup for maximum growth.

Chapter 15: Take advantage of being unknown

It's hard for me to imagine entertainment before TV shows on DVD and Netflix. I love binge-watching shows that I never got around to watching on live television. In early 2013, my wife and I decided to give the NBC comedy *Parks and Recreation* a second try. We had watched part of the first season a few years back and couldn't get into it, but when we picked it back up again, I got to watch the show through the lens of Citizinvestor and the work we were doing with city governments just like the City of Pawnee. The show follows the life of Leslie Knope (played by Amy Poehler) – a comically passionate government employee who serves as the Deputy Director of Parks and Recreation for the fictional City of Pawnee, Indiana.

One night, my wife and I were watching the show when we saw Leslie Knope walk across the screen to a poster of a fundraising progress bar and say, "I need $35,000, but the city doesn't have enough money in its budget."

"Oh my gosh, this is Citizinvestor!" Kara said.

I couldn't believe how perfectly the show was making the case for our startup. The project Leslie Knope was advocating for (turning a dangerous pit into a community park) was the perfect case study for Citizinvestor. Leslie had engaged citizens to get feedback on the idea and cut through the requisite red tape at City Hall to secure approval for the park. She only lacked one thing: the $35,000 she needed in the City's budget to bring the park to life. It was perfect! Even the dollar amount for the fictional project was in the ballpark of our average project size on Citizinvestor.

As I talked through the parallels with Kara, she could see the wheels turning in my head. She knew I was up to something. I checked my calendar and to-do list for the next day and found that I had a relatively open schedule. When I sat down at my laptop the next morning, I began searching *Parks and Recreation* scripts for keywords relevant to Citizinvestor. As I began ripping clips of the show off shady video-sharing websites, I called Tony.

"I need you to put your attorney hat on," I told Tony.

"Umm sure," he said, afraid of where I was taking the conversation.

I explained to Tony that I wanted to take video clips of the show and piece them together to make a video pitch for Citizinvestor, all without the consent of NBC.

"What's the worst NBC can do?" I asked Tony.

"They may send us a cease and desist letter," he replied. "But they aren't going to sue us."

Secretly, I was hoping NBC *would* send us a cease and desist letter, as I knew that if the letter were made public, it would only draw more attention to Citizinvestor. But we knew this was unlikely. We were a startup, and nobody outside our little universe was paying any attention to us. And in this case, that was a good thing. We decided to take advantage of being unknown.

The video turned out *way* better than we had anticipated. We never considered producing one of those animated how-to videos you see on every startup's website as we thought most of them looked cheap and didn't do a good job telling the story behind the products. What we came up with was far better than any of these animated shorts. Even though it used clips and characters from a fictional TV show, we had something that told a story about a very real problem every government entity faces. Here's how the script turned out:

Narrator: Meet Leslie Knope.

Leslie Knope: Hi I'm Leslie Knope, Deputy Director of Parks and Recreation.

Narrator: Pawnee, Indiana is like most cities in the United States, with hundreds of projects the government would like to take on.

Leslie Knope: I'm trying to turn a giant dirt pit into a community park.

Narrator: Some of these projects have a lot of support from citizens.

Leslie Knope: Would you support turning that lot into a community park?

Citizen 1: I'm all for a park.

Citizen 2: A park, huh? That seems like a good idea.

Narrator: So, the good people in local government go to work to make these ideas a reality.

Leslie Knope: OK, brainstorm, how do we make this park happen?

Tom Haverford: Let's go to the City Council directly and ask them to put up the money.

Leslie Knope: No, parks are not a priority.

Narrator: Unfortunately, local government budgets are tighter than ever before.

Leslie Knope: I need $35,000, but the city doesn't have enough money in its budget.

Narrator: So, these shovel-ready projects sit on a shelf collecting dust because they lack the necessary funds to complete.

Leslie Knope: Sigh.

Narrator: Until now. Citizinvestor works with municipalities like the City of Pawnee to allow citizens to crowdfund the civic projects they care most about!

April Ludgate: That's a genius move.

Narrator: Thanks! It's our way of helping citizens get the projects and services they want at a time when government has no other way to pay for them. To learn more, visit Citizinvestor.com. That's...

Leslie Knope: Citiz...

Tom Haverford: investor...

Ron Swanson: dot com.

With the video locked down, we spent weeks thinking through the best way to release it. We decided to unveil it just before our panel at SXSW (the popular interactive, film, and music festival held annually in Austin, TX) in an email sent to the Citizinvestor community "From: Leslie Knope."

The email and video looked so legit that dozens of people asked us how we were able to convince the NBC producers to film a promo video just for us. For months, we were on the lookout for a letter from the attorneys at 30 Rockefeller Plaza. That letter never came.

In a startup, you have so many things stacked against you. While you're relatively unknown, use that position to your advantage. Think outside the box, ask forgiveness instead of permission, and take risks you won't be able to take as your company matures.

Chapter 16: Stay humble and accessible

When we launched Citizinvestor, we laid out strict rules for who could and who could not crowdfund projects on the site. We were pitching the site as "a crowdfunding platform for local government projects" to differentiate ourselves in an already crowded (forgive the pun) market of crowdfunding platforms, most of which allowed anyone to raise money for anything. This wasn't the only reason we vetted project creators though. We believed that by requiring projects to have a sponsoring government entity, they would have a greater chance of being completed if successfully funded on the site. Even though we explicitly stated this rule for posting projects on the site, we were constantly being contacted by individuals wanting to raise money on their own without a sponsoring government entity. The volume of these requests was piling up to the point where we were tempted to let many of these emails go unanswered; but Tony and I made a commitment early on that as Co-founders of the company, we would personally respond to every email that came through to us. That rule of accessibility was the only thing that kept us from leaving one such email from a high school student in Eugene, Oregon, unanswered:

> My name is Isaac Meyer, and I am a student at Sheldon High School in Eugene, OR. I am the president of Green Club, a student-led environmental awareness group at the high school. We would be interested in crowdsourcing to fund improvements to the bicycle rack parking area. This would include adding more bicycle

parking, as well as replacing some racks that only allow the front wheel of the bike to be locked, leading in multiple cases to bike theft or vandalism.

While a high school Green Club is a far cry from a government entity, we took the time to thoughtfully respond to Isaac's email. As Tony worked with Isaac, we discovered in these high school students an incredible story of civic engagement. It turned out that Isaac and his friends had approached the Eugene School District to request the funds they needed to replace the old bike racks on the campus of Sheldon High School. But the School District didn't have the funds needed to purchase the bike racks. Googling his way out of this problem, Isaac found Citizinvestor and, after learning that our projects required a sponsoring government entity, went back to the School District and convinced them to crowdfund the project on our platform. Once the project was posted, Isaac and his friends worked harder than anyone else we've seen to raise their funding goal. In less than three days, they had raised 100% of their goal – a record time that has yet to be beat on Citizinvestor. While Isaac and his friends got new bike racks for their campus, we got another incredible story to tell about the power of crowdfunding civic projects. Isaac and his friends became our poster children for how engaged citizens could use Citizinvestor to create real change in their cities. But if we had arrogantly ignored Isaac's email, brushing him off as just some random high school student, we would have really missed out.

The point here isn't that you have to respond to every single email you're ever sent. The point is to stay humble and accessible. Personally responding to every email that is sent through the general contact form on our site is just one way Tony and I stay accessible, but it certainly isn't the only way. This value of staying accessible manifests itself in a number of practical ways:

- We refuse to outsource customer service. The Co-founders of Citizinvestor respond to every question, bug report, feature request, etc., that come through the site.
- We personally respond to every media request, regardless of how small or large a publication's readership is.
- We rarely turn down requests for the founders to share our experience at conferences, panels, or other speaking engagements.
- We always accept invitations to talk to university students inside and outside of class.
- We make the personal email addresses of each of the founders easy to find.

I wholeheartedly believe that when you are in the startup phase of a company, the founders and the company's brand are interchangeable. Because of this, it is impossible for people to feel like they can connect with your company if they cannot connect with you. If you are asking people to connect with your vision, your product, and your brand, ensure that you are making it as easy as possible for them to connect personally with you. To do that, you have to be humble and accessible.

Some of my favorite startup founders exemplify this well. Dennis Crowley, the Co-founder and CEO of Foursquare, has been known to tweet out where he'll be watching Syracuse basketball games, asking fans to join him. As *Fast Company* wrote of Crowley in August 2013, "his true social grace is his underlying humility. At a tech gathering in Brooklyn, a wide-eyed attendee didn't recognize Crowley and asked what he did. 'I work at a tech startup,' he replied."

Zappos' core value – "be humble" – shines through in CEO Tony Hsieh's must-read book *Delivering Happiness*. In the book, Hsieh explains that every Zappos employee – even senior executives – spends their first weeks at Zappos manning phones in the company's call center learning how to respond to customer needs. As CEO, Hsieh's desk is no different than any other employee's at Zappos (a trait he and Crowley share).

As the introduction to ABC's hit show *Shark Tank* explains, Mark Cuban is a "notorious billionaire entrepreneur, tech guru, and the outspoken owner of the NBA's Dallas Mavericks." Yet with all of Cuban's fame and fortune, he remains accessible to hungry entrepreneurs by making his email address public and frequently responding to cold email pitches.

These successful entrepreneurs offer an example to follow. While there have undoubtedly been moments in which we thought we were too big for our britches at Citizinvestor, we try our best to stay humble and accessible. Not only is this best for those around us, but it also opens the door to amazing opportunities that we may otherwise overlook.

Chapter 17: Rely heavily on interns

In the fall of 2013, Tony and I were overwhelmed by Citizinvestor's growth. We had more cities posting crowdfunding projects than we knew what to do with and we knew we needed help to get the projects funded. While we had awesome interns work at Citizinvestor in the past, we had never given them direct responsibility to help get projects funded. But this semester, we were forced to rely more heavily on our interns than ever before, so we decided to try something new. We split the crowdfunding projects on Citizinvestor in half and gave our two interns a single directive for the semester: Do everything in your power to get "your" projects funded. Almost immediately, an incredible spirit of competition took root with the interns who were now in constant battle with each other to come up with the most creative and effective campaigns to help get their projects funded.

One of these interns, Daniel Kahn, came to me one afternoon with an idea he had to promote "his" project in Central Falls, Rhode Island. The project (which you will learn much more about in Chapter 19) was raising money to replace the flimsy plastic trash cans in a public park with steel trash and recycling bins in an effort to permanently improve the city's trash problem. Daniel wanted to organize a cleanup day at the park to temporarily fix the city's trash problem and raise awareness of the crowdfunding campaign. I immediately loved the idea, so Daniel emailed our contacts at the City to see when we could schedule the cleanup day. The City quickly responded to tell us that they wanted to do the event in 2½ weeks. There was just one seemingly big problem with that plan: I was less than 24 hours away from a two-week vacation to Hawaii with my wife. I told Daniel that if we were going to do this, he would have to plan, organize, and promote the event all on his own. Daniel didn't even flinch. He was up to the task.

Before I left the office for vacation, I made a list of the myriad of things Daniel would need to do in order to pull the event off. Here are just a few of the items I put on Daniel's plate:

- Coordinate with the City's Director of Parks and Recreation on meeting time, location, tools for the cleanup, etc.
- Design a flyer to promote the event
- Invite neighboring college fraternities, sororities, and clubs to attend
- Set up a sign-up form for the event and a short URL to promote the form offline
- Email reporters from *The Boston Globe* and other major news outlets to convince them to come and write about the cleanup

When I boarded the plane for vacation the next morning, I wasn't worried at all about Daniel's ability to get the job done. I expected him to be able to get about 20-40 people to the cleanup, which we all would have been thrilled with. When I got back from vacation, Daniel was still frantically working to increase turnout. I had decided to fly up to Central Falls to witness the event for myself and answer reporters' questions about the City's first Citizinvestor project. When I pulled up to the park for the cleanup, I couldn't believe my eyes.

More than 100 people in this city of only 19,000 people showed up to clean up the park. Trying to put the turnout in perspective, I did some quick math on my phone: This was the equivalent of 43,000 residents of New York City volunteering to clean up Central Park! We had placed a tremendous amount of responsibility in Daniel's hands, and he far exceeded our expectations.

This shouldn't have surprised us. This is just one example of how we consistently place a great deal of trust in our interns. Almost every time, they knock our expectations clear out of the park.

In a startup, you will be overwhelmed by the amount of work you have to get done. Before hiring paid help (if you can afford it), find a local university and offer unpaid internships to students. And don't think you have to be Google, Facebook, or The White House to get top-tier talent to come intern with you for free. Every semester, we are able to attract top-notch students to work at Citizinvestor for no pay. Here's how I think we do it:

- We rely heavily on interns, giving them lots of responsibility and treating them as Co-founders of the company. Interns do much of the same work the Co-founders of the company do and are privy to almost every one of our conversations.
- We have fun in the office, pitting interns against each other in competitions to see who can successfully fund the most projects.
- We take our time during the hiring process for each class of interns, making sure that each one is smart, competent, and fits within our culture.
- We always try to make the internships more

valuable for the interns than for us, constantly asking each intern for feedback on which areas of the company they want to focus on and giving them the freedom to pursue projects they are passionate about.
- We give our interns the opportunity to solve a real problem. I believe this is key to understanding millennials and their approach to work. In almost every interview we conduct with candidates for Citizinvestor internships, the interviewee articulates that they want to work somewhere that makes a difference. They want to work for a company that is solving a very real problem.

I once had a professor at The University of Tampa email me to say that "unpaid internships have become a thing of the past." That's not what the market says! You don't have to be a well-known institution to attract great interns. You just have to be solving a real problem and be willing to place a lot of trust and responsibility in these highly motivated and capable students. By relying heavily on interns you will attract amazing unpaid talent and in turn give them invaluable experience for their career.

Chapter 18: Have the audacity to ask

There are few books written by politicians that are worth reading. But when I saw that California Lieutenant Governor Gavin Newsom was publishing a book called *Citizenville* about "how ordinary citizens can use new digital tools to [change] our relationship with government," I knew I had to pick it up. As I cracked open the book, I couldn't believe how perfectly it fit with the work we were doing at Citizinvestor. Newsom challenged his readers with the following:

> Why not set up a system whereby people can donate $3 or $5 or however much they want—DonorsChoose-style—to help pay for government projects? What if cash-strapped cities and states in need of funding for things like road repairs or providing free public wi-fi or upgrading their DMV's computer system simply asked citizens to donate specifically towards these projects?

"They are," I verbally exclaimed from my couch. "This is *exactly* what we're doing at Citizinvestor!" It was as if Newsom and I were in a mind-meld, thinking identically about how to solve one of the most important problems facing cities. Although polar opposites politically, Newsom and I appeared to be kindred spirits in our thoughts about solving big problems in local government.

Most people read things like this, note how cool they are, and then flip the page to the next chapter. Not me. As soon as I read those words, I opened up the to-do list app on my phone and added a new project: "Meet with

Gavin Newsom re: Citizinvestor." There was no reason for me to think I *should* get a meeting with the Lieutenant Governor of the State of California, but based on my experience, I knew I *could* and I was shameless enough to try. Some people may think this is arrogance. I think it's audacity, and I would argue it is one of the most important qualities for any entrepreneur to have.

After a quick Google search, I found Gavin Newsom's email address and shot him the following note:

> **Subject:** the Donors Choose for government
>
> Lt. Governor Newsom,
>
> My name is Jordan Raynor and I am one of the Co-founders of **Citizinvestor** – a crowdfunding and civic engagement platform for local government projects.
>
> My Co-founder (CC'd) and I are huge fans of the work you are doing and of *Citizenville*. As we were reading through the book, we came across a passage in which you called for a DonorsChoose for government. We believe we have built just that in Citizinvestor.
>
> We would love the opportunity to meet with you to explain our platform in more detail and get your feedback on the work we are doing. Please let us know if you might have an hour or so in the coming months to chat with us.

Within days, the Lieutenant Governor's team responded to say that they would try to make the meeting work. But after two months of trying to get something on his calendar, the trail went cold. It was time to call a play I knew to be tried and true. I had a conference scheduled in San Francisco July 30-August 2, 2013, so I used this as an excuse to follow up with Newsom's team and give them hard dates for when I would be in Northern California. I hadn't heard from his team in two months, but this email elicited a response the next day confirming a date, time, and location that the Lieutenant Governor would meet with me. Pro tip: If you really want to schedule a meeting like this but don't have an excuse to be in the same city as the person you're trying to meet with, make one up. Giving them firm dates you are "planning on being in town" makes it more likely that they will give you a hard yes or no.

When I arrived at the cafe the Lieutenant Governor chose to meet at, I was pleasantly surprised to discover that it was directly across the street from his first entrepreneurial endeavor, Plumpjack Wines. Instead of launching right into my pitch of Citizinvestor, I asked as many questions as I could about his first startup, soaking in the wisdom he shared as he reminisced on a career 20-plus years in the making. Once we got talking about Citizinvestor, he was quickly fired up. Newsom was the former Mayor of San Francisco, so he was intimately familiar with the problem we were trying to solve. Halfway through my PowerPoint deck, he opened his phone and called a number of his contacts at City Hall, asking them to meet with me right away. After 40 minutes or so of sipping tea and talking politics, startups, and mutual friends, I was in a cab heading to City Hall to walk through the doors my new friend had just opened.

Gavin Newsom is just one of the remarkable people I have been able to meet in my short career. Like I said at the beginning of this book, a big reason why I have been able to gain access to these people is because of the "real problems" I have attempted to solve. But that's not always enough. Sometimes you have to have the audacity to ask for meetings, introductions, or favors you "shouldn't" get. You have to be able to ask yourself "Why not me?" Why can't you get a meeting to pitch a dream client, an interview with your dream employer, or a coffee to meet someone you respect? When you ask for these things that others shy away from, I think you'll find more yeses than you expect. In my experience, I've found that some of the most successful people are also some of the most accessible and willing to help.

Chapter 19: Don't sell products, tell stories

While I was in Tampa for another infamously humid summer, Tony was spending six weeks in beautiful Rhode Island visiting family. This was a tradition for Tony and his family, one that I had learned to live with as his startup spouse. Our long-distance relationship meant fewer trips to Lin's Hibachi Buffet and more time on Google Chat. One chat in July 2013 started one of the greatest stories we have had the pleasure of telling at Citizinvestor:

> **Tony:** Central Falls RI just signed up on site and emailed me
> scheduling a call later today
>
> **Jordan:** sweet
>
> **Tony:** could be good press ... one of the only US cities to go bankrupt
> could have nice redemption angle
>
> **Jordan:** wow
> would be amazing press
> lock
> it
> down
>
> **Tony:** will do
>
> **Jordan:** GO meet with them!
> How far away are they?

Tony: gonna offer it
its RI nothing is over 30 minutes away

    For more than a year, Tony and I had been selling our product to cities touting our technology, success rate, and the fact that Citizinvestor was free for cities to use. My academic background is in public relations, so I'm constantly looking for the stories behind my companies. While we had some good stories to tell to accompany our pitch of Citizinvestor, we had yet to find "the one." Tony and I would constantly talk about the need to "find our Pebble" – a reference to the paper watch that crowdfunded more than $10,000,000 on Kickstarter.com. The Pebble quickly became shorthand for an amazing story of the promise of crowdfunding. As soon as the City of Central Falls signed up for Citizinvestor, we instinctively knew that we held our own precious pebble in our hands.
    In 2010, Central Falls became the first city in Rhode Island history to file for bankruptcy. Two years later, the Mayor resigned his post due to charges of corruption. If any group of citizens had an excuse to distrust and disconnect from government, it was the people of Central Falls. Following the Mayor's resignation in 2012, the City elected his successor, 27-year-old James Diossa, with the daunting task of leading the City out of bankruptcy and restoring trust between City Hall and its citizens. And now they were looking to Citizinvestor to help do just that.
    Of the hundreds of cities we have pitched Citizinvestor to, we have only met with a handful of them in person. But because Tony was already in Rhode Island, it was a no-brainer for him to meet with the

Mayor and his staff in Central Falls. When Tony called to brief me on the meeting, he informed me that Stephen Larrick, our main point-of-contact in Central Falls, had assembled all of the department heads to attend the meeting and offer ideas for projects the City could crowdfund on Citizinvestor. Someone pointed out that when the Mayor asked students what they wanted him to focus on, they overwhelming asked that he clean up the trash that littered the one-square-mile city. The students had identified the trash as a source of shame for their city. Knowing that much of the litter originated from the flimsy trash cans that were easily knocked down in the park next to City Hall, Larrick devised a plan to replace the bins with trash and recycling bins made of steel. But the City didn't have the $10,044 they needed to make the project happen. The Mayor, Larrick, Tony, and the department heads came to a consensus that crowdfunding these trash bins would be the perfect first project on Citizinvestor. After the meeting, Larrick emailed Tony to say that, "Since the bankruptcy, it's been rare to see our department heads excited and willing to share positive ideas, so the excitement they showed yesterday over Citizinvestor was very encouraging."

I couldn't have asked for a better story to tell; and the major media outlets agreed. CNBC published one of my favorite headlines about the launch of Central Falls' first Citizinvestor project: "Issue municipal bonds? No thanks, we'll crowdfund instead." TheVerge.com told the story beautifully, saying that "economically strapped cities around the country can't afford basic improvements. If Central Falls meets its goal, it could serve as a model for other municipalities to follow."

These were the talking points we had been pushing for months, but it took a great story for the concept to be understood by the masses.

The amazing cleanup day our intern Daniel organized helped visualize in the physical world what Citizinvestor was all about: empowering citizens to invest in their community. These citizens were telling a powerful story of civic engagement by investing their time *and* their money to restore their city. A few weeks after the cleanup event, the front page of *The Boston Globe* ran a story on how the City's efforts on Citizinvestor were helping Central Falls establish "a new identity, as a model of creative, modern, interactive government." Soon after the story was published, the project reached its goal of raising $10,044 to install the steel trash bins.

Front page of The Boston Globe

With our beautiful pebble in hand, we showed it off to anyone who would listen. Months after the project reached its funding goal, Mayor Diossa wrote an op-ed to *The Providence Journal* saying that the "citizens who contributed to our first Citizinvestor project demonstrated the deepest level of civic engagement," and that the City of Central Falls is now "a model for what civic engagement should look like in the 21st century."

To this day, in nearly every speaking engagement, media interview, and pitch to a city, we make sure to tell the incredible story of Central Falls. In a startup, it's easy to get in the habit of selling your product's features, how it works, and why it's a great value. While all of these things are important, I have found that they are secondary to telling great stories. Stories inspire us. They paint a picture of what is possible. Do everything you can to find, cultivate, and share the story you want told about your company.

Chapter 20: Stand for something

In the early days of Citizinvestor, one of the most common questions we received from news media, investors, and friends was how Citizinvestor was different from Kickstarter, the most well-known crowdfunding platform at the time. While it was never our intention to directly compete with Kickstarter, there were some obvious similarities. We even introduced Citizinvestor as "the Kickstarter for government projects" in our original pitch decks. But we knew that if we were seen as a Kickstarter competitor, we would lose. They were Goliath, and we were David while he was still tending sheep. In a document outlining our original strategy for demonstrating that we were not playing in the same space, Tony wrote that Kickstarter was "very pure in their purpose of only funding creative projects and they have shown no signs of wavering from that commitment" by getting into the crowdfunding of government projects. When we tested the line with investors and news media, it fell flat.

    For months, we iterated our answer to this question. One night, Tony and I were having a beer with Russ Wallace, the founder of a startup very similar to Citizinvestor that had just shut down. As we were all sharing in our excitement for how transformational crowdfunding could be to the way citizens get public projects, I referred to our users as "micro-philanthropists" and explained how with $5 or $10, anyone can be "a modern day Carnegie or Rockefeller," financially contributing to a public good. Russ loved it and urged me to use the line everywhere we went. That week, I tested out the messaging for the first time, tweeting "At @Citizinvestor we are creating a community of micro-philanthropists. Will you be one?" People loved it! I knew we were on to something. A few weeks later, Kickstarter offered up a golden opportunity for us to hammer home our new messaging and take a stand that would clearly differentiate Citizinvestor.

When we launched Citizinvestor, we did not include the "rewards" feature that Kickstarter had become known for. Kickstarter's rewards-based model of crowdfunding allowed project creators to give t-shirts, hats, and limited editions of products to users who contributed a certain amount to their crowdfunding campaign. Over time, Kickstarter took criticism for essentially becoming a shopping platform where hipster technology enthusiasts would come to purchase the next cool thing. The company was even forced to respond to the growing criticism in a blog post titled "Kickstarter Is Not a Store."

Seeing an opportunity to both differentiate Citizinvestor and rally our fans, I eagerly awaited a reporter to ask me why we did not offer rewards for donations to project as Kickstarter did. I didn't have to wait long. In an emailed response to the question, I told one reporter, "I love shopping on Kickstarter, but we are building an entirely different community of people: a community of micro-philanthropists passionate about investing in their community, who with $5 or $10 can financially contribute to the building of public projects. The difference between Kickstarter and Citizinvestor is the difference between get and give."

The messaging stuck and when we began sharing it with Citizinvestors (a term we prefer to "users"), it turned them into raving fans of our company. To this day, Citizinvestors constantly ask us to send them Citizinvestor stickers to put on their laptop. Some send us pictures of them proudly wearing their Citizinvestor t-shirts in public.

Our community treats Citizinvestor as a movement, not a product. I believe they do this because we stand for something as a company. While the concept of micro-philanthropy is a great marketing term to help distinguish us from other crowdfunding platforms, it also serves a larger purpose in communicating a value of living generously that is core to who we are as founders and a company.

No company is agnostic. Every founder has values that are in one way or another woven into the fabric of their company. In his classic book, *Built to Last*, author Jim Collins calls these "core values" and defines them as "the organization's essential and enduring tenets – a small set of general guiding principles not to be compromised for financial gain or short-term expediency." Defining core values may seem like a process reserved for massive corporations, not young startups. I thought so too until I read the inspiring example of Sony's Founder, Masaru Ibuka, who in the rubble of a post-World War II Japan did "something remarkable for an entrepreneur wrestling with the problems of day-to-day survival…He codified an ideology for his newly founded company."

In late 2013, Tony and I made the decision to further define Citizinvestor's core values to show our community and the world what we stood for. Here they are:

Live generously
We believe that generosity makes us better citizens. One who lives generously seeks to put others above themselves, freely giving their time, energy, and resources.

Love where you live
No one likes the guy who hates his hometown. Every city is broken, we know that. But we believe we are called to *love* where we live.

Be audacious
Dream bigger. Have a healthy disrespect for the status quo. Never fear failure.

Be disciplined
Vision without discipline is false hope. We love lists and focus, because we know that's what makes us most free to do the best work.

Be self-aware
We know what we're good at and what we suck at and we love that quality in others.

Transparency
Not lying is not enough. True transparency is in the best interest of everyone from customers, to employees, to partners.

Always be learning
Our love of learning spills into everything we do, from running constant experiments on our products, to A/B testing messaging, to always having a book in our hands.

For good, for profit
Profit and social impact are not mutually exclusive. We believe the best way to create real change is by creating new value in the marketplace.

When we first shared these core values with the world, the reaction was overwhelming. Citizinvestors shared the values they identified with most via social media. Bloggers whom we had never spoken to began covering news about the company. Influential people in our network emailed us to let us know they were "with us." Your customers, fans, followers, investors, partners, and every interested party in between wants to know what your company stands for. Tell them, and they will turn your company into their cause.

Epilogue

I don't know how the story of Citizinvestor will end. There's a chance the company will outlive my Co-founders and myself. There's a chance that we will be acquired for a "life-changing" amount of money. There's a chance that we will fail. For better or worse, this uncertainty is one of the defining characteristics of entrepreneurship. But regardless of what happens to Citizinvestor or any of my future endeavors, I will be content because my startups don't define me. They aren't my life's purpose.

As a Christian, I find my ultimate hope in God's promises like the one found in Jeremiah 29:11 which says "'I know the plans I have for you,' declares the Lord, 'plans to prosper you and not to harm you, plans to give you hope and a future.'" My faith gives me eternal purpose and hope that will survive any business failure or success. I believe this is the key lesson I've learned on how to be an effective entrepreneur. In business, everyone has their share of success and failure. If your startup is your source of significance, you will be rocked from the highest of emotional highs to the lowest of emotional lows. Finding your hope in something other than your startup is essential.

As you turn the last page of this short book, I hope you walk away with some valuable advice on how to launch a company, grind through startup life, and grow your business. I hope the stories stick with you for years, helping you avoid some of the mistakes I've made and encouraging you on your path as an entrepreneur. Finally, I hope you found this book valuable enough to share it with a friend who you think could benefit from having heard these stories and lessons.

In the spirit of accessibility, I invite you to email me anytime at jordan@jordanraynor.com. I would love to hear your comments and questions about the book or your own stories from your experiences as an entrepreneur.

Acknowledgements

Much like building a great company, I have learned that writing a book is a team sport. There are so many people who played a role in shaping this work. To each of you, I say thank you. But some deserve special acknowledgement here.

First, I must thank my beautiful bride, Kara. In hindsight, starting this book in the middle of your pregnancy probably wasn't the wisest decision; but as always, you have been incredibly gracious and supportive every step of the way. I love you more than life itself and am so excited about this next chapter of our story.

To my startup spouse, Tony: Thank you for asking me to take this journey with you. Here's to many more years of success, Chinese buffets, and platinum Taylor Swift albums.

To the rest of the founding team at Citizinvestor (Erik, Mathias, and Nick): Thank you for betting on this idea to transform the way citizens and government interact.

To Marci Harris, Story Bellows, Steve Ressler, Patrick Ruffini, Russ Wallace, and every informal advisor to Citizinvestor: Thank you for your invaluable counsel as we have built the foundation for this movement.

To Dave Wistocki, Chelsey Keenan, Daniel Kahn, Kat Poblete, Evan Moore, Micah Barker, and Ansley Kahn – the rock-star interns of Citizinvestor. Thank you for sharing your time and considerable talents for our cause. I hope your internships were more valuable to you than they were to us.

To Jeff Madsen, Bryan Ickes, Joe Nammour, and every other contractor that has helped make Citizinvestor what it is today, thank you.

To every citizen who has ever donated to a Citizinvestor project or used our platform to propose an idea: Thank you for investing in your community.

To my good friends and some relative strangers who gave this book a first pass, thank you for shaping this work: Clay Brown, Chris Johnson, Tyler Burton, Jordan Casal, and Alberto Peralta.

To Krystal Whitten who greatly improved my vision for the cover of this book and brought it to life, thank you for creating something so beautiful.

Finally, I want to thank God for giving me these stories to tell. I am completely undeserving of the grace and opportunities You give me each day.

About the Author

Jordan Raynor is a serial entrepreneur who has spent his career using technology to solve real problems in politics, government, and business. He is a Co-founder of Citizinvestor – the largest crowdfunding platform for government projects in the United States. He is also the Founder of Vocreo – a digital agency that helps other entrepreneurs and leaders use the Internet to achieve their goals.

In 2011, Jordan's first company was "acquihired" by Engage – deemed a "mega-interactive agency" by Mashable. At Engage, Jordan's team lead digital strategy for some of the most high-profile politicians in the world including Paul Ryan, John Boehner, and Tim Pawlenty. In 2013, Jordan was named one of four appointees to the State of Florida's User Experience Task Force. He has twice been selected as a Google Fellow and served as a White House intern in 2006. A highly sought-after public speaker, Jordan has spoken at major events such as TEDx, SXSW, the World Forum for Democracy, and The Guardian's Activate Summit.

Jordan is a sixth generation Floridian currently residing in Tampa, Florida with his wife, Kara.

Made in the USA
Lexington, KY
09 August 2014